Expansion through Financial Management
and the effective use, or rather non-use, of cash.

Meshulam Riklis

All rights reserved. No part of this publication may be
reproduced, stored in a retrieval system, or transmitted in any form or by any means, electronic,
mechanical, photocopying or otherwise, without the prior permission of the copyright owner.

The views and ideas expressed in this book are the personal opinions of the author, and do not necessarily
represent the views of the Publisher.

© Copyright 1966 by Meshulam Riklis

Published by Rentech Books

rentech@mailfence.com

EXPANSION THROUGH FINANCIAL MANAGEMENT CASE STUDIES

A Thesis

Presented in Partial Fulfillment of the Requirements
for the Degree Master of Business Administration

by

Meshulam Riklis, B. A.

The Ohio State University
1966

TABLE OF CONTENTS

                                                                                         Page

LIST OF TABLES iv

CHAPTER

I. INTRODUCTION .... 1 - 2

      Financial Management - The key to External Corporate Expansion

II. BEGINNING AN ACQUISITION PROGRAM .... 3 - 25

      Initial Research Endeavors
      First Application of the Theory (Gruen Watch and Smith-Corona)
      My First and Lasting Control Base is Established (The Rapid Electrotype Company and American Colortype Company)
      Investment in Butler Brothers

III. HISTORY OF ACQUISITIONS LEADING TO PRESENT CORPORATE COMPLEX .... 26 - 34

      Sale of Butler Brothers
      Purchase of United Stores Corporation and Subsequent Merger of United Stores Corporation-B.T.L. Corporation and McCrory-McLellan Stores Corporation into McCrory Corporation
      Purchase of Oklahoma Tire & Supply Company
      Acquisition of H.L. Green Company, Inc.
      Acquisition of Lerner Stores Corporation

IV. PROBLEMS AND REHABILITATION .... 35 - 48

      Integrating Our Past Acquisitions
      Problems with McCrory-McLellan-Green Division
      Rapid-American's and McCrory's Problems
      The Rebuilding Process both Internally & Externally (Glen Alden Corporation)

CHAPTER		Page
V.	CASE STUDIES	49 - 72

        The Rapid Electrotype Company
        United Stores-B.T.L. Corp.-McCrory-McLellan
          Merger
        Oklahoma Tire & Supply Company
        Lerner Stores Corporation
        Our Corporate Structure Today and its
          Future Direction

VI.	SUMMARY AND CONCLUSIONS	73 - 79

        Prerequisites for Mergers and Acquisitions
        Formation of Objectives
        Use and Non-Use of Cash

BIBLIOGRAPHY 80

LIST OF TABLES

TABLE		PAGE
I.	Rapid Electrotype Company Balance Sheet As of December 31, 1954	9
II.	Smith-Corona, Inc. Balance Sheet As of June 30, 1955	11
III.	American Colortype Company Balance Sheet As of December 31, 1955	15
IV.	Rapid-Electrotype-American Colortype Pro-Forma Balance Sheet As of December 31, 1956	16
V.	Butler Brothers Balance Sheet As of December 31, 1956 and Operating Highlights 1951-1956	19
VI.	Butler Brothers Balance Sheet As of December 31, 1958	27
VII.	McCrory Corporation Recast Pro-Forma Balance Sheet (giving effect to merger of B.T.L., United Stores & McCrory-McLellan) As of March 31, 1960	29
VIII.	McCrory Corporation Balance Sheet As of December 31, 1962	31
IX.	Rapid American Pro-Forma Balance Sheet As of January 31, 1962	36
X.	Rapid American Balance Sheet As of January 31, 1964 and Pro-Forma Projected January 31, 1967	42
XI.	Oklahoma Tire & Supply Company Balance Sheet As of December 31, 1959	57
XII.	Reconciliation of McCrory's Cost for Oklahoma Tire & Supply Plus Cash Flow Derived from Oklahoma 1960-1965	59

LIST OF TABLES Cont'd.

TABLE		PAGE
XIII.	Lerner Stores Corporation Projected Contribution to McCrory Year Ending January 31, 1967	67
XIV.	Present Corporate Structure	69

CHAPTER I

INTRODUCTION

Financial management is perhaps the most potent factor in successful development of prosperous business corporations in our time and offers a unique opportunity to capable aggressive businessmen to build large and strong industrial concerns from relatively modest beginnings. Quite often today financial management concentrates more on directing expansion and growth of a company through acquisition of and merger with another business. While it may seem quite natural and not too difficult for a corporation to enlarge its scope and increase its volume by acquiring another company either wholly or in part and merging the two into a stronger entity, there are numerous business operators who have learned from experience how difficult it is to make the right choice, to devise the correct formula making the acquisition or merger beneficial to both seller and buyer, and to make the corporation more viable and useful in further expansion.

The story told in the following pages points out, I believe, the existence of unusual opportunities for personal and corporate progress through financial management. I have taken the liberty of relating the stories of various acquisitions and mergers in the first person because they present my personal experience, as I have been privileged to be the prime mover in all these activities. However, one can easily see the underlying general principles in carrying through these mergers and the guiding lines that have contributed to the successful conclusion of the deals. It is suggested that the reader further study the basic principles of this intriguing subject by reference to "Security Analysis" by Graham & Dodd.[1]

---

[1] New York; McGraw Hill Book Co., Inc. 1951

CHAPTER II

BEGINNING AN ACQUISITION PROGRAM

John Ruskin once said that education is the leading of human beings to what is best, and making what is best out of them; that this is attainable by the training which makes men happiest in themselves and also makes them most serviceable to others.

My training began at Ohio State University combining the influence of all the courses without knowing which of them was most important and, therefore, concluding that all were equally valuable.

No wonder, therefore, when Dr. Gilbert Riddle asked me to research and find a company that had more cash per share than the price of the stock in the "market" I was completely awed not knowing where to look. However, after I had solved that technicality by referring to a downtown brokerage firm, I detected that such situations existed and in considerable numbers. I actually found a whole industry - cement - where almost every company answered Dr. Riddle's query.

"Why?" I kept asking myself.

I could not find a reason "why", and might note here that fifteen more years living with these questions have yet to yield the answer. But I found a great desire to get involved in and lead such a company myself to see whether

I could change its course.

I began to dream about what I would do with a large cash position if I were in charge of such a company. I realized then that one must have control of a company in order to turn such dreams into reality. Control! This was the word that was going to ring through my ears for the next few years. I realized, though, that I had a lot more to learn.

I started as a junior analyst at Piper Jaffray and Hopwood of Minneapolis in the fall of 1951 and was amazed at the number of publications and information sheets that were available on almost any subject or any company and especially at the amount of material that was flowing out of the research departments of the big New York houses. I then became more intrigued to search for the "sleeping beauties" since almost every day one could read somewhere about "undervalued situations". However, to invest was not what I had in mind - but rather to take a company out of its slump and build it into a company of strength.

I began my research by a study of the economy and the forces that made for its growth. I studied and analyzed, industry by industry - from retail organization to mining, from steel to oil, from automotive to farm implements. Hundreds of annual reports of companies passed through hands along with their proxy statements. After a time, I acquired the ability of thumbing through them, absorbing the essentials and differentiating between the important and the unimportant.

My thoughts now turned in two directions - both of which combined later to form the basis of this paper...

(1) With the perusal of proxy statements and annual reports, I noticed many companies whose previously aggressive managements and owners had either passed away or grown old only to find the second generation incapable or unwilling to face the new challenges, thus allowing for a purchase of a controlling interest.

(2) With the study and analysis of industry by industry and company by company within the industry, I came up with a dream of building, through mergers and by acquisitions, a "Giant" complex.

I became engrossed in a dream about possible acquisitions of such situations, evaluating the potential of those companies under new management and their expansion via mergers and acquisitions. It was like a phantom chess game that I played with unknown partners.

I had now arrived at a principal decision never to

go into any deal of merger or acquisition if it does not immediately offer by itself a chance for further growth. In simple words this means not to pay cash for a company that cannot immediately generate at least a similar amount of cash for the next move. If, however, such an acquisition is desirable, but cannot produce the cash, then it has to be acquired via another method of financing.

"Control" and "Expansion" were now fully planted in my mind. Numerous special situations were tucked away in my files but I now found that there was a third element that was missing - money to start the program.

I became a securities salesman feeling that I could now devote my time to gathering and educating potential customers for special situations under their control and for expansion.

It took me another year before I could put together a special situation syndicate. Almost three quarters of a million dollars was committed plus the right of the syndicate to borrow an equal amount and so at the end of 1954 I was able to lead our group in successful negotiations for the controlling block of Gruen Watch Company of Cincinnati. My position with the group was clearly defined. I was now to plan, execute and generally assist in the diversification program.

I had high expectations for Gruen Watch. I was hoping that under a new president we would immediately cut the losing government contract operations and concentrate on the watch business. I suggested contracting for watch movements in a fashion similar to that used by other U. S. watchmakers and to effect the sale of the Gruen factory in Switzerland in order to generate some five million dollars for further acquisitions and diversification.

I advocated such plans, but had no part in the daily management and was snubbed by the president in his desire to run things his way. The group in Minneapolis, my money source, began to quarrel and spent a lot of time undermining each other's position leading to the disintegration of the group and I severed connection with Gruen.

This setback showed me clearly that the next time I must not be content with being a member of the group and advising it on negotiations and acquisitions but must also lead the group and be responsible for both the diversification and acquisition and the daily management of its affairs.

I began looking for another situation. In researching all the stocks that were listed on the Cincinnati Stock Exchange I came across the Rapid Electrotype Company that had a net worth of about $2,800,000; a very small capitalization of approximately 124,000 shares; and about 10% of the stock concentrated in the hands of the chairman of the board, who was at that time seventy years old. The company had a very strong cash position and annual earnings of about $200,000 after taxes. It had hardly any money invested in fixed assets or inventory. Furthermore, its inventory and receivables were turning over every 30 days. I could see that the entire cash position of about $2,000,000 might be available for further acquisitions and diversification. See Table I for a statement of conditions of the Rapid Electrotype Company as at December 31, 1954.

I approached the chairman of the board of Rapid Electrotype on behalf of a syndicate and finally agreed on a price of $28.00 a share which was almost $10.00 above the then current market price of the stock. The same offer was made to all shareholders.

I was elected chairman of the board at the end of 1955 and devoted thirty to sixty days to reviewing the company's operations, I visited all the plants, discussing procedures with the plant managers, and undertook a number of steps to improve the profit participation of the managers as well as the company's profits. Other incentives in the form of a stronger profit-sharing plan and a stock option plan were also initiated in order to induce the

TABLE I

THE RAPID ELECTROTYPE COMPANY

BALANCE SHEET
AS OF 12/31/54
(in $ millions)

ASSETS

CURRENT ASSETS:

Cash & Equivalent	1.6
Notes & Accounts Receivable	.5
Inventories	.3
Total Current Assets	2.3
Net Plant	1.1
TOTAL	3.4

LIABILITIES

CURRENT LIABILITIES:

Accounts Payable	.1
Accrued Liabilities	.5
Total Current Liabilities	.6
Common Stock & Surplus	2.8
TOTAL	3.4

managers to get the best out of their subordinates. Much was achieved in the next year and the earnings of the company increased 50%.

Simultaneously with these improvements, I directed my attention to a diversification program, which I felt would be the most significant for the future of the shareholders. After studying all available information, I decided that I would start with the electronic and data processing industry and therefore with a typewriter company, since it is the base for many data processing projects. Smith-Corona Inc. attracted my attention because: [2]

1. It had a small capitalization of a little over 300,000 shares.

2. Its book value was greater than market.

3. Its earnings were impressive, even though erratic at times.

4. Its trade name was good and could be utilized further in the office equipment field.

Most important was the block of stock already accumulated by Gurdon Wattles (about 20%) which might be for sale. I approached Mr. Wattles and made a deal to buy the stock for the account of Rapid Electrotype at a cost of almost $1,500,000.

Management of Smith Corona had previously considered

---

[2] See Table II for statement of conditions of Smith Corona Inc.

TABLE II

SMITH-CORONA INC.

BALANCE SHEET
AS OF 6/30/55
(in $ millions)

ASSETS

CURRENT ASSETS:

Cash	1.5
Trade Accounts & Notes Receivable	5.8
Inventories	10.6
Total Current Assets	18.0
Investments	.1
Net Plant	7.3
Prepaid Expenses & Deferred Charges	.5
Goodwill, Trademarks & Formulae	.9
TOTAL	26.8

LIABILITIES

CURRENT LIABILITIES:

Notes Payable	.4
Trade & Other Accounts Payable	.7
Accrued Expenses	1.5
Taxes Payable	.4
Total Current Liabilities	3.3
Long-Term Debt	7.9
Reserves	.3
Common Stock & Surplus	15.3
TOTAL	26.8

and rejected an opportunity to buy Kleinschmidt Laboratories - an electronic company selling solely to the government and manufacturing teletype machines and related items. Urged by one of the directors, I looked into the Kleinschmidt situation and was immediately impressed with this company's potential growth, able management, good facilities, and its possible coordination with Smith Corona.

Even the price asked by the sellers was reasonable at that time ($2,300,000 for a company earning $600,000-$800,000 after taxes). At this point it was easy to bring about a change of opinion on the part of the board of Smith Corona, which voted around May of 1956 for the acquisition of Kleinschmidt.

This was Smith Corona's first move toward diversification and acquisition. It greatly encouraged me and I did not hesitate, therefore, to increase our interest in the company until it reached close to 40% of its equity.

However, this move alerted the Smith Corona management to the fact that I intended influencing the future of the company and its direction. Despite my friendly attitude toward the management, they sought to fend off the intrusion of an outside influence in their company.

The acquisition of Kleinschmidt gave management an excellent opportunity to do exactly that. The price for

Kleinschmidt was changed from cash to 80,000 shares of Smith Corona, and a pre-alerted board of directors met in July of 1956 to change the already voted deal to a new one. I objected, but the new acquisition was steamrolled through with a battery of lawyers watching every move and every resolution.

The new shares would increase the total outstanding shares to about 400,000 and dilute our block to a little less than 30 percent of the outstanding stock. It also brought another block of 20 percent into being.

We appealed to the courts, but a referee rejected our plea. The only other solution was a proxy fight. I had neither the ambition for a proxy fight nor the desire to stay on where we were not wanted. By September of 1956 we arranged to sell our block of Stock at a profit.

I had some satisfaction in later years upon seeing that Smith Corona did indeed proceed to acquire and expand (Marchant Calculator-1957) but its management was soon dismissed and completely replaced with that of Kleinschmidt's and its headquarters changed from Syracuse to New York City. However, I have learned never again just to sit by with controlling interest of a company without affirming this control by a majority representation on the Board of Directors.

Not very long after the purchase of Smith Corona stock by Rapid Electrotype, I was approached by Gurdon Wattles to find out whether we were interested in any of the assets of American Colortype, a company listed on the New York Stock Exchange and 50% owned by one of his companies.

American Colortype had 250,000 shares outstanding and a book value of over $12,000,000. Its holdings consisted of a printing company, a Christmas and other card company, a metal sign company, some real estate and other assets. See Table III for statement of condition of American Colortype Company.

My reasoning for my interest was that if we could buy the 50 per cent offered and then merge with Rapid in some form, we could achieve two things in the process:

1. Based on the projected acquisition, we could probably sell some equity security of Rapid Electrotype Company and increase its net worth.

2. We might be able to increase Rapid's net worth further by issuing a subordinated long-term obligation for the balance of the stock and thus add to Rapid the leverage of this debt and the difference between the cost price and the larger book value. See Table IV, consolidating statement of Rapid Electrotype and American Colortype

TABLE III

AMERICAN COLORTYPE COMPANY

BALANCE SHEET
AS OF 12/31/55
(in $ millions)

ASSETS

CURRENT ASSETS:

Cash	1.3
Receivables	4.9
Inventories	4.1
Total Current Assets	10.3
Receivable On Sale Of Assets	.6
Net Plant	5.0
Deferred Charges & Other	.1
TOTAL	16.0

LIABILITIES

CURRENT LIABILITIES:

Serial Notes	.2
Accounts & Other Payables	1.6
Accrued Liabilities	.6
Total Current Liabilities	2.4
Serial Notes Due 1962 (paid 2/1/57)	1.4
Federal Income Taxes Due 1958 to 1963	.2
Common Stock & Surplus	12.1
TOTAL	16.0

PRO-FORMA BALANCE SHEET
(Giving Effect To Merger Of American Colortype)
AS OF 12/31/56
(in $ millions)

ASSETS

CURRENT ASSETS:

Cash & Equivalent	2.8
Receivables	4.9
Inventories	2.9
Total Current Assets	10.6
Investment	.3
Receivable From Sale Of Assets	1.0
Deposit On Purchase Of Equipment	.5
Net Plant	5.3
Deferred Charges	.1
TOTAL	17.7

LIABILITIES

CURRENT LIABILITIES:

Notes Payable - Banks	1.5
Serial Notes (paid 2/1/57)	1.4
Accounts Payable	1.3
Accrued Liabilities	.8
Total Current Liabilities	4.9
Federal Income Taxes Due 1958 to 1963	.4
5-½% Two-Year Debentures, Due 5/1/58	.7
7% Sinking Fund Subordinated Debentures	4.9
Common Stock & Surplus	6.8
TOTAL	17.7

proforma, December 31, 1955.

In April of 1956, we purchased the 125,000 shares of American Colortype for about $4,500,000, 60% of it paid in cash and the balance due in six months. I intended merging Rapid Electrotype and American Colortype fast and thus having the credit of both companies to back the second payment. However, this merger was later delayed for a year because of the adverse publicity during our attempt to control Smith Corona. Still, for the first payment on the shares of American Colortype purchased we borrowed $1,000,000 from the bank and sold $1,600,000 of convertible debentures. The final payment coincided with the sale in September 1956 of the Smith Corona stock for about $2,000,000. The management of the affairs of American Colortype was taken over immediately and I set out on a program of cash generation. The real estate and other assets were sold and all divisional operations were tightened. It took only four months before we generated close to six million dollars of cash in American Colortype.

Thus, in 1956 the Rapid Electrotype Company was doing well financially, owing only a million dollars to the banks, but controlling 51% of American Colortype which, in turn, had over six million dollars cash in the bank. Management of four different divisions (one in Rapid and three in American) was to occupy a great deal of my attention. Consolidation of our operations and development of a management cadre became the project for the next three years in the later merged Rapid American Corporation.

Just then an opportunity presented itself to move toward expansion again. After some study and reflection I decided to seize this opportunity. It was in the fall of 1956 that I was approached by a fellow director who wished to interest me in taking a position in Butler Brothers. Butler Brothers Company was at one time a reputable name in the wholesale distribution of dry goods catering to retailers. Now composed of five major distribution centers, it was supplying merchandise to independently owned, but franchised, variety store owners under the name of Ben Franklin.

Butler Brothers also owned a variety chain of eighty stores in the Midwest - Scott Stores - and a chain of five department stores on the West Coast, operating under the name of Butler Brothers. Sales were approaching two hundred million dollars and profits seemed to be increasing. See Table V for statement of condition and profit statements of Butler Brothers.

I met with the management and some dissident directors and was impressed and interested. However, there were two

BALANCE SHEET
AS OF 12/31/56
(in $ millions)

ASSETS

CURRENT ASSETS:

Cash & Equivalent	8.1
Receivables	13.9
Merchandise Inventories	15.2
Prepaid Expenses, etc.	.6
Total Current Assets	37.9
Net Plant	3.4
TOTAL	41.3

LIABILITIES

CURRENT LIABILITIES:

Accounts Payable	6.7
Federal Income Taxes	2.7
Other Accrued Expenses	2.7
Total Current Liabilities	12.1
Common Stock & Surplus	29.3
TOTAL	41.3

OPERATING HIGHLIGHTS 1951-1956
(in $ mil, except per share figures)

Y/E 12/31	TOTAL SALES	PRE-TAX NET	NET INC	EARNINGS P/Sh
1956	124.5	5.3	2.5	2.47
1955	114.9	5.1	2.5	2.12
1954	119.0	3.5	1.6	1.14
1953	125.7	2.6	1.2	.73
1952	117.5	2.8	1.3	.76
1951	114.1	4.3	1.9	1.31

questions to be answered.

1. What was the potential for the future?

2. Would control be in contention?

I was satisfied as to the management ability, and, in retrospect, I can only add that they were one of the finest and most honorable groups that I had dealt with in my total experience.

In answering my second question, I was given assurances that with an acquisition of some 200,000 shares American Colortype Company would get at the next shareholders' meeting the numerical majority of representation on the Board of Directors.

We proceeded to buy for the American Colortype Company approximately 200,000 shares. Butler's management and directors made good their commitment in April of 1957. There followed three wonderful years of association with Butler's President A. O. Steffey, Chairman Emil Schram and their top group of executives. Mr. Steffey's warm relationship and cooperation and assistance made up for many differences that existed on both sides, and caused the company to move forward for growth and progress, resulting in higher sales and profits. Despite my fine relationship with Al Steffey and the smoothness with which our operations ran, we received a cold shoulder in the local banking community and were never able to establish a strong and lasting banking connection in Chicago. It may have been this, subconsciously, that eventually led to our sale of Butler Brothers and the move to relocate our interests.

Our program in the parent companies shifted to one of consolidation and management build-up. The year of 1957 saw Rapid Electrotype make an exchange offer for the balance of the American Colortype shares. This offer was in the form of a high coupon straight debenture. As a result over 85% of the stock was then acquired by Rapid. At the end of 1957 a full merger of the two was voted to establish Rapid American.

We also proceeded to sell the printing division and increase our stock ownership of Butler Brothers to 51%.

All the efforts and know-how in acquisitions was shifted to the expansion of our Christmas Card Division into school supplies and gift wrap paper. This division, The American Paper Specialties, eventually grew to a $20,000,000 annual sales and profits of about $1,000,000 before taxes. Early in 1962 this division was sold to a corporation whose major shareholders were the management group of this division and a group of outside investors. The consideration was $5,000,000 in cash and $7,000,000 in notes that were to be repaid with a public sale of some of its securities. The division changed its name to APS Corporation.

A new division was formed in the field of discount mail order by the acquisition of two mail order companies - one in the Midwest and another in the East.

In the field of management build-up I envisioned a combination of three factors: (1) advancement of our own people in management procedures and operations; (2) the creation of a reservoir of top operating and executive talent, (3) the establishment of a team of experts that could roll in and out of a specific situation and be able to diagnose and solve its problems.

With this aim, I created a "Central Management Staff" - a team of experts in the various fields of management, particularly industrial, but not limited to it. They came from colleges and management advisory firms that specialized in the teaching of management techniques and in analyzing and helping companies in their reorganizations. In total they numbered about six or seven at the peak of the program.

The Central Management Staff was to report only to me, and together we set out to do the job for which they were chosen.

A. A study was undertaken of each division and each plant within the division. The studies were discussed and conclusions for improvements reached. A member of the staff was then sent to the division to help and to implement the recommendations.

In addition company-wide seminars on management courses were initiated. These had the additional object of introducing our various top level people to each other and were as a rule concluded by my presentation on the direction that our company intended taking.

B. Members of the staff were encouraged to assume active roles in the divisions to which they were assigned, so they could be transformed into actual division heads when it became necessary. From the beginning they were told that their ultimate work was to be in active leadership and not just in consulting.

C. In choosing people for this staff I tried to assemble a homogeneous group, but one with a diversity of expertness: Industrial engineers, inventory control experts, administrative planners and others. I hired a small auditing company so that I could use its people for financial and internal auditing control.

Close cooperation was also established with our legal and tax advisors to complement the industrial and financial control, particularly in the workings of our early stages in the acquisition program.

In short, during those three years we did well financially by keeping our biggest investment - Butler Brothers - well protected and its management happy; consolidating and generating cash and profits in our parent company and building a strong team of management, both for the present and the future.

I became aware in 1957 that Roger Babson, who controlled McCrory-McLellan Variety Stores through United Stores, was looking for a buyer for his holdings. He had now controlled these companies for over twenty years and he and the management were not getting any younger.

Toward the end of 1957 I was able to conclude a deal, whereby Rapid was to purchase control of United Stores and with it McCrory-McLellan. These companies were doing about a quarter of a billion dollars in business annually and their earnings were going down. However, at the last minute, Mr. Babson changed his mind and in early 1958 sold the control to Bankers Securities of Philadelphia.

Bankers Securities kept the company a little over a year. In early 1959 it was bought by H. L. Green, itself a variety retail chain. This company had just been merged and taken over by Maurice Olen, a young industrialist from Alabama.

In the middle of 1959 a discrepancy was found in the books of Olen's company, after it merged into H. L. Green and the board of his company requested and received his resignation amid a great furor that undermined the ability of H. L. Green to operate successfully. This event also disturbed the operations of its controlled subsidiary, McCrory-McLellan Stores.

I followed these events very closely and was quite familiar with the McCrory-McLellan operations. I could envision the creation of a large diversified merchandising entity with McCrory-McLellan as a cornerstone.

CHAPTER III

HISTORY OF ACQUISITIONS LEADING

TO PRESENT CORPORATE COMPLEX

To be in a position to acquire McCrory-McLellan I sought to sell the assets and business operation of Butler Brothers Company and use the cash proceeds for the future program. The only drawback to this plan was the possibility of losing the listing on the New York Stock Exchange as well as the chance of being classified as an investment company. To avoid this, we had to move rapidly with our program of acquisitions.

After some negotiations, we concluded in November 1959 the sale of the assets of Butler Brothers for approximately $50,000,000. The closing of the transaction, subject to shareholders' approval, was set for February, 1960. See Table VI for Butler Brothers statement of condition as of December 31, 1958.

Thus started "Operation Big Switch", as we called it at the time.

Within ten days after receipt of our money in B. T. L., which was the shell left from the sale of assets of Butler Brothers, we bought control of United Stores, which, in turn, controlled McCrory-McLellan. In the process, we accumulated about 10% of H. L. Green. Not knowing whether

TABLE VI

BUTLER BROTHERS

BALANCE SHEET
AS OF 12/31/58
(in $ millions)

ASSETS

CURRENT ASSETS:

Cash	4.7
Receivables	14.8
Merchandise Inventories	23.2
Prepaid Expenses, etc.	1.4
Total Current Assets	44.2
Net Plant	7.6
Intangibles	6.4
TOTAL	58.2

LIABILITIES

CURRENT LIABILITIES:

Accounts Payable	10.6
Federal Income Taxes	2.8
Other Accrued Expenses	4.2
Total Current Liabilities	17.6
Installment Notes	6.5
Minority Interest	1.2
Common Stock & Surplus	32.9
TOTAL	58.2

they would sell United Stores, I decided it was safer to work on both "fronts". This controlling interest acquired in McCrory-McLellan, and the part interest of H. L. Green, were the cornerstones upon which we could now start building the new merchandising company.

First, we moved to eliminate the two holding companies - B. T. L. Corporation, the depository of cash, and United Stores, the controlling company of McCrory-McLellan. A merger of the three companies was effected swiftly in July of 1960. See Table VII which outlines the consolidating effect of such a merger and the securities issued in exchange.

Next, we concluded the acquisition of Oklahoma Tire and Supply Company, a regional chain of automotive stores concentrated in the Mid-South. A month later, we acquired National Shirt Shops, a small but well-managed chain in the field of Men's and Boys' furnishings.

In early 1961, we also concluded the acquisition of control of Lerner stores, the largest and best known women's wear chain, and at the request of H. L. Green's management bought for cash over 50% of that company via a tender offer.

Toward the end of 1961, we added the small Economy Stores chain to the operations of Oklahoma Tire and completed the merger of H. L. Green into McCrory Corporation, the name

McCRORY CORPORATION
RECAST PRO-FORMA BALANCE SHEET
Giving effect to merger of
United, B.T.L. & McCrory-McLellan
AS OF 3/31/60
(in $ millions)

	McCrory-McLellan	United Stores	B.T.L.	Consolidating Adjustments & Eliminations	McCrory Corporation
TOT INV CAP	62.8	10.3	46.3	(22.3)	97.1
L.T. Debt	.5	-	-	-	.5
Preferred	6.0	8.0	-	1.5	15.5
Common Equity	56.3	2.3	46.3	(23.8)	81.0
Represented by:					
CURRENT ASSETS (including)	39.6	.7	33.5	(3.3)	70.5
Cash & Equivalent	4.1	.4	33.1	(3.3)	34.4
Less:					
CURRENT LIABILITIES	20.2	.1	.8	-	21.2
WORKING CAPITAL	19.4	.6	32.7	(3.3)	49.3
Add:					
INVESTMENTS	.6	9.4	13.5	(19.0)	4.6
NET PLANT	39.9	.1	-	-	40.0
OTHER ASSETS	3.1	.3	.2	-	3.5
	43.6	9.8	13.7	(19.0)	48.1
Deduct:					
DEFERRED TAXES	.2	-	-	-	.2

CAPITALIZATION: (# of Shares in Thous.)

	McCrory-McLellan	United Stores	B.T.L.	Consolidating Adjustments & Eliminations	McCrory Corporation
PREFERRED					
3½% Cum CV ($100 Par)	60(a-1)				60
$6 Cum CV Prf ($100 Par)					96
UNITED $6 Cum CV Prf ($25 Stated Value)		96(b-1)			
UNITED $4.20 Non Cum 2nd Prf ($5 Par)		1,126(b-2)			
COMMON	3,367(a-2)	513(b-3)	1,023(c-1)		5,434

TERMS OF EXCHANGE

McCRORY

(a-1) For each share of 3½% Cumulative Convertible Preferred Stock, par value $100 per share, convertible into five shares of Common Stock, liquidation preferences $104 (voluntary) and $100 (involuntary) per share, callable at $104 per share.

One share of 3½% Cumulative Convertible Preferred Stock, par value $100 per share, convertible into five shares of Common Stock, liquidation preferences $104 (voluntary) and $100 (involuntary) per share, callable at $104 per share, of the Surviving Corporation.

(a-2) For each share of Common Stock, par value $.50 per share.

One share of Common Stock, par value $.50 per share, of the Surviving Corporation.

UNITED

(b-1) For each share of $6 Preferred Stock, without par value, convertible into one share of Common Stock, liquidation preference $115 per share, callable at $115 per share.

One share of $6 Cumulative Convertible Preference Stock, par value $100 per share, convertible into three-fourteenths of a share of Common Stock, liquidation preference $100 per share, callable at $115 per share, of the Surviving Corporation (subordinate as to dividends and in liquidation to the Preferred Stock of the Surviving Corporation).

(b-2) For each share of $4.20 Second Preferred Stock, par value $5 per share, convertible into one share of Common Stock, liquidation preference $75 per share, callable at $75 per share.

Three-quarters of a share of Common Stock, par value $.50 per share, of the Surviving Corporation.

(b-3) For each share of Common Stock, par value $.50 per share.

Three-fourteenths of a share of Common Stock, par value $.50 per share, of the Surviving Corporation.

B.T.L.

adopted after consolidation. A tender offer by McCrory Corporation to the balance of Lerner's shareholders brought over 90% of the stock and in the end McCrory owned about 98% of Lerner Stores. H. L. Green sold its Canadian subsidiary, Metropolitan Stores, in early 1961, and later fully merged into McCrory to form with McCrory-McLellan one operating division in the variety field (known now as M M G). See Table VIII giving financial condition of McCrory Corporation as of January 31, 1962.

It may be of interest to review the methods used in these acquisitions devised to fit the ability to finance them and preserve the future growth of McCrory Corporation.

<u>July, 1960</u> The merger of United Stores, McCrory-McLellan Stores and B. T. L. was achieved mainly by common stock, with the exception of the 6% preferred of United, which continued as such, and McCrory-McLellan preferred stock, which was exchanged for a similar preferred stock.

<u>October-November, 1960</u> The acquisition of Oklahoma was for cash and ten-year notes ($10,000,000 in cash and $18,000,000 in notes). The cash was generated by the sale of the company's receivables and did not cause any drain on McCrory's cash position.

ASSETS

CURRENT ASSETS:

Cash	20.6
Accounts & Other Receivables	15.3
Merchandise Inventories	95.9
Prepaid Expenses	2.4
Mortgages Receivable	1.7
Total Current Assets	135.9
Net Plant	85.1

OTHER ASSETS:

Excess Of Purchase Cost – Lerner Stores	17.2
Debenture Discount	9.4
Deferred Charges & Other	5.3
TOTAL	253.0

LIABILITIES

CURRENT LIABILITIES:

Current Maturities of Long-Term Debt	3.0
Accounts Payable	36.1
Accrued Expenses & Sundry Liabilities	17.9
Accrued Federal Taxes On Income	3.7
Total Current Liabilities	60.7
Long-Term Debt, less current maturities	62.9
Deferred Taxes & Other	5.6
Minority Interest	3.0

SHAREHOLDERS' INVESTMENT:

Preferred Stock	24.6
Common Stock & Surplus	96.3

The National Shirt Shop acquisition was partly for cash, and the balance by a small issue of convertible preferred stock. The cash was replenished by the excess cash held by National Shirt Prior to the merger.

February and Late 1961 Lerner Stores was acquired mainly by the offer of a fifteen-year debenture and warrants. Most of this issue is still outstanding.

May and Late 1961 Half of H. L. Green was purchased for about $22,000,000 in cash and the other half for convertible preferred stock and warrants. Most of the cash was regenerated from the sale of the Canadian subsidiary and the liquidation of the Olen Stores.

November, 1961 The Acquisition of Economy Stores was for cash amounting to less than $2,000,000.

Early in 1960, with the outline of our program well-developed I turned to the task of seeking an experienced and talented man who could head this diversified combine of retailing companies. After due inquiries and investigation, I offered the position to a fairly young, aggressive and very-well-thought-of merchandising executive from Sears Roebuck and Co.

He joined our company in the Fall of 1960 to become President and Chief Operating Officer and his immediate program was (1) to rejuvenate the ailing variety division, (2) to merge the H. L. Green operation with McCrory-McLellan and (3) to coordinate these with the other divisions (Oklahoma, National Shirt and Lerner) for the benefits that could be derived from such joint ownership.

While McCrory Corporation was consolidating its corporate structure and operations in 1961, I realized that Rapid-American was dwarfed by its huge subsidiary. Rapid American had diluted its ownership of McCrory after the merger in 1960 of B. T. L., United and McCrory-McLellan and now owned 32% of the outstanding stock of McCrory Corporation. Its net worth was less than one-fifth of McCrory's and any future consolidation (based on 51% ownership) must be preceded by making Rapid a larger and stronger company. To this end we acquired in Rapid American by the issuance of common stock three companies, all well-managed and good earners.

In mid-1961, we acquired Cellu-Craft, a flexible packaging company with sales of about $10,000,000 and after-tax profit of about $350,000. In November 1961, we acquired a Citrus Grove and packaging operations with sales of about $8,000,000 and earnings of over $300,000 after taxes. In early 1962, we acquired a group of children's clothes manufacturing companies, with sales of about $8,000,000 and earnings of about $300,000 after taxes. The total consideration in these acquisitions amounted to a little over 400,000 shares of common stock of Rapid American.

CHAPTER IV

Problems and Rehabilitation

What was the future likely to be? In the middle of 1962 the situation presented an enthusiastic picture.

Rapid American had a good combination of diversified companies and a strong management team, gathered together from within, brought in from other companies in similar fields, or gained with the acquisitions, its management comprising substantial stockholders, greatly interested in the future success of the company. Employee benefits were raised to standards almost unheard of, in the desire to make them all conscious of their membership in one "family".

The financial conditions of Rapid American were strong with projected cash flow based upon the sale of American Paper Specialties Division and the programmed sale to the public, sometime in 1963, of a participation in the Cellu-Craft Company. In addition to the above, Rapid American concluded in late 1961 and early 1962 the sale of fifteen-year debentures in the amount of $10,000,000. See Table IX giving a proforma statement of conditions of Rapid American as of July 1962.

As to McCrory, it now presented a fully merged and integrated management. McCrory-McLellan-Green (variety

PRO-FORMA BALANCE SHEET
(Giving Effect To Sale Of Notes Due
From American Paper Speciality Co.)
AS OF 1/31/62
(in $ millions)

ASSETS

CURRENT ASSETS:

Cash	12.8
Accounts & Notes Receivable	6.4
Inventories	7.5
Prepaid Expenses, etc.	1.2
Total Current Assets	28.0
Investments (Principally McCrory)	31.2
Net Plant	5.7
Other Assets & Deferred Charges	1.1
TOTAL	66.1

LIABILITIES

CURRENT LIABILITIES:

Accounts Payable	7.2
Currently Maturing Debentures & Notes Payable	4.3
Accrued Liabilities	1.3
Total Current Liabilities	12.8

OTHER LIABILITIES:

7% Sinking Fund Subordinated Debs Due 11/15/67	4.0
5-3/4% Convertible Subordinated Debs Due 1/1/77	8.4
4½% - 6% Notes Due 1963-1976	13.5
	25.8
Common Stock & Surplus	27.5
TOTAL	66.1

division) was now combined under a new task force with at least six or seven ex-Sears Roebuck's seasoned functionaries, four of whom were once supervisors (a position equivalent to that of Vice President in the merchandising department of Sears Roebuck & Co.) Operating management was now in its second year and extremely enthusiastic about its past and future accomplishments. Lerners was doing better than ever, new store openings were accelerated and cash flow was strong. Oklahoma Tire and National Shirt Shops were also doing better.

Our enthusiasm was at an all-time high when the stock market took its worst setback in mid-1962, which we saw as a blessing in disguise, allowing Rapid American to complete our program and acquire 51% of McCrory Corporation

My thinking was prompted by the feeling that we probably would never again be able to buy McCrory stores as reasonably, in view of its growth of earnings. I was convinced that McCrory would command a much higher multiple and grow in geometric rather than in arithmetic progression because it possessed the required elements of:

1. Management – operating and financial;

2. Money – excess cash for growth; and

3. Net Worth – equity of almost its price.

By October 1962, Rapid American spent about 30 million dollars in cash and equivalent to buy about 1,500,000 shares of McCrory. It now owned 51% of McCrory but no cash resources whatever. Rapid American investment in McCrory Corporation now grew to about $44,000,000. Over half of this investment was of the most recent vintage at higher prices and almost all of it secured the various loans made to Rapid American.

Unfortunately, McCrory's earnings for the year ending January 31, 1963 were issued in early April, 1963 and turned out to be disappointingly less than half those projected by the operating management. This seemed to trigger and accentuate a number of difficulties.

Most serious was the effect on McCrory's credit standing. No company can truly operate without the support of good credit. This is even more so in a retail organization where buildup towards Christmas business enhances the need for confidence by the vendors and by finance companies and factoring concerns supplying the financing for the vendors. The results of fiscal 1962 and the dismissal in mid-1963 of the operating management created havoc both within and without. Added to it was the discovery that the cash position, so strong in the past, had deteriorated considerably with poor sales and lack of earnings and with very high inventory and costly fixed plant expenditure.

It took me weeks before I was finally able to evaluate the situation and cope with the serious dilemmas that were facing us.

My analysis showed the following:

Rapid ... Most acute was the pressure of money. The value of the McCrory stock investment was down from $55,000,000 to $28,000,000 and in terms of cost was down some $15,000,000. Short-term debt was very heavy against the operations, and even though most of the term debt was in good shape there was a small amount of it becoming due shortly and fast approaching default unless it could be extended and modified.

The projected cash flow was not realistic any longer, making any modification very difficult unless the company indicated a willingness to do everything possible to secure and repay its debt.

McCrory ... Here the problems existed in many areas and, therefore, the timing of their solutions was also important. The two most significant ones were:

1. Danger of credit squeeze, particularly with "Back to School" and "Christmas" business approach-

ing... inability to receive goods at suitable prices could have permanently damaged the company.

2. The Variety Division was completely demoralized from the point of view of personnel. The entire cadre of top executives resigned or was dismissed. Inventories were high, liquidity low, and losses mounting.

There were other problems demanding immediate attention. I naturally concentrated on solving the most pressing problems first.

Rapid ... the decision was self-evident: everything must be liquidated, leaving only 51 per cent of McCrory. The future of Rapid was to be tied stronger than ever to the fortunes of McCrory for good or bad. Negotiations ensued, sometimes very tedious, until finally the stockholders of Rapid approved in November of 1963 the sale for cash and notes of three major divisions: Citrus - back to its original owners; Cellu-Craft - back to its original owners, and Children's Wear - to a syndicate organized by one of our directors. The Mail Order Division was liquidated; the Metal Division was liquidated, and a couple of the original Rapid Electrotype plants were sold. Only one plant remained, in San Francisco.

It was now clear to our banks and financial institutions that we were doing our utmost. So, they helped next by modifying, for six months only, our term debt and whatever was left from the short term debt. At the end of six months, in mid-1964, and with McCrory on its way to recovery, everything was again extended for two years and later modified further and extended to meet with our projected earnings and cash flow. See Table X comparing Rapid American financial statements as of January 31, 1964 with proforma January 31, 1967.

McCrory Corporation ... In order to alleviate the fear of a potential credit squeeze, and with no time to concentrate on the cash generation from within, we offered to sell our Lerner Stores Company to Glen Alden Corporation. This was met with strong opposition by our shareholders and caused us to face the most bitter attack on our financial integrity.

When the smoke cleared, although the shareholders rejected this plan, we gained valuable time to study and launch a program aimed at an operational and financial recovery. The major officers of Rapid, now freed from any duties there, joined me in McCrory for this task. Operationally, a major study of the ills of the M M G Division was

TABLE X

RAPID-AMERICAN CORPORATION
Balance Sheets, January 31, 1964
And Pro-Forma Projected January 31, 1967,
With McCrory Carried As An Investment
Rather Than Consolidated
(in $ millions)

ASSETS

	1964	1967
CURRENT ASSETS:		
Cash	1.1	3.8
Other	1.0	14.9
	2.1	18.8
Investments: (Principally McCrory)	46.3	43.8
Property & Equipment - Net	.3	1.1
OTHER ASSETS:		
Excess Of Purchase Cost	1.5	12.1
Sundry	2.4	2.2
TOTAL	52.6	77.9

LIABILITIES AND SHAREHOLDERS' EQUITY

	1964	1967
Current Liabilities	3.1	13.0
Long-Term Debt	38.0	34.6
Other Non-Current Items	.8	1.5
SHAREHOLDERS' EQUITY:		
Preferred Stock:		
Par Value $1.00, Annual Dividend $.75, Issued 850,932 Shares	-	.9
Par Value $10.00, Issued 150,000 Shares	-	1.5
Common Stock:	2.1	2.1
Par Value $1.00, Outstanding 2,101,707 Shares		
Capital Surplus	14.3	21.0
Earned Surplus	(5.0)	5.7
	11.8	31.2
Less: Equity In Subsidiaries Cost Of Its Treasury Stock	1.1	2.4
Total Shareholders' Equity	11.8	31.2
TOTAL	52.6	77.9

undertaken, and a plan of rehabilitation developed. It concentrated on the "field" or direct operational control over the stores.

We started from one store, then applied the same measures to a group of stores (a district of seventeen) and then to an entire region of 100 stores. When this was well on its way the other regions joined in. The program was aimed at personal contact with the store, district and regional management - and their training in working together to improve quickly profitable results or to control losses. Incentive programs were put into effect which eventually resulted in tremendous improvements in control of inventory shrinkage and expenses. With improvements in the field operations well under way, the emphasis shifted to the home office. The major effort was to improve buying and re-organize the distribution of goods. This M M G division returned to about $7,500,000 profit in 1964 and then to about $9,500,000 in 1965.

Financially, we concentrated on cutting out all excess weight, firming up our credit standing by getting a revolving credit of $57,000,000 for six months and then renewing $50,000,000 for two years.

Next we concentrated on generating back the cash from

inventory and by selling National Shirt Shops. When we completed this entire phase, by the second half of 1964, we found ourselves with some $20,000,000 to $30,000,000 in "free" cash that could be used in operations. Free, because of our assured credit, it could now be used for investment outside the retailing field.

With financial and operational recovery on its way, our problem in 1964 still lay in the after effects of 1963 difficulties. The image of our company had been marred by the events of 1963, and I realized that, in order to turn this leaf, our program in the next twelve months must be to lay the foundation for a stronger company both financially and in management.

I knew that one year was not enough. We now had to show that McCrory's earnings were here to stay and that our program could not again be halted because of lack of management. In addition, our program had to encompass the financial and operational rehabilitation of Rapid to provide it with growth and earnings from within and not only through McCrory.

McCrory also faced the task of now using its money for a program of diversification and for growth in its retailing direction. Expansion of its present facilities was as important as diversification if we were to prove that we could continue to keep the ball rolling.

If we were to achieve further growth by acquisition, we had to prove that coming to "live" with us was a privilege rather than a burden. I realized that a favorable public image could not be gained by the hiring of a good public relations firm, but could only be sustained by proof of stability and growth. It is with the above in mind that I began to negotiate with my friend, Mr. Albert List, with a view to purchasing control of Glen Alden Corporation in McCrory Corporation.

Glen Alden by itself was a diversified company with interests in coal mining, leather tanning, movie theatres and textile mills. In addition, it had substantial cash and cash equivalents.

I could see that liquidation of some of the assets and the rehabilitation of its theatre operations could bring in more cash and improve earnings. I could also see the psychological effect on other companies and their managements by proving that the association of Mr. Albert List with our company lifted us from a "leper colony" status to a place of respectability.

Negotiations were concluded toward the end of 1964 and the same offer of cash and short-term notes were tendered to all Glen Alden Corporation shareholders. McCrory Corporation ended with a 49.7% interest in Glen Alden Corporation. The total investment was about $25,000,000 cash and $10,000,000 in five-year notes.

The year 1965 improved our public image. Glen Alden Corporation became a very profitable company after it sold its leather and coal mining operations. It rehabilitated its theatre division so that that division became the biggest producer of profit in times return on invested capital. Glen Alden Corporation also produced something like $40,000,000 in cash and another $15,000,000 in cashable items.

A 30% interest in Philip Carey was acquired by Glen Alden Corporation in early 1966 and a merger announced. Other moves are planned in the future along with further strengthening of textiles and theatres. The company produced earnings of about $6,000,000 with no tax in 1965; it will probably repeat the same in 1966. After the merger with Philip Carey Manufacturing Company - and with full taxes - it is likely to produce the same in 1967. This result is projected without the advantage of the use of its cash resources that are mainly kept in certificates of deposit and other cashable items.

McCrory too expanded further in retailing by its entry into the promotional department store field with the acquisition of first a minority and then a majority of S. Klein Department Stores, Inc. of New York. This giant retailer was suffering from indigestion and insufficient management and capital to cope with a company which expanded rapidly from three to ten stores.

S. Klein Department Stores, Inc. is now undergoing a complete reorganization and is likely to provide McCrory with another test of management skill. As soon as certain technical problems can be resolved, a program of additional stores, now being planned to be financed by McCrory, will be added to those existing.

Cash flow in McCrory Corporation was further augmented by the offering to the public of 40% of Lerner shares. McCrory now owns only 50% of Lerner Stores Corporation but has never been as strong financially as it is today. Exclusive of its investment in Glen Alden Corporation, McCrory's cash improvement since 1963 amounts to over $40,000,000.

Last but not least has been the search for, and

finally the purchase by Rapid American of, a manufacturing company with earnings of over $4,000,000. In December of 1965, Rapid acquired Joseph H. Cohen & Sons, Inc. for $21,000,000 in cash and notes, $9,000,000 of which was loaned to Rapid by commercial banks.

Taking advantage of this purchase, and the more secured future of Rapid, we were at once able to sell $5,000,000 of preferred stock and also merge into Rapid, for preferred stock, another company that had cash and liquid assets of over $8,000,000. See Table X for proforma statement of conditions of Rapid American, January 31, 1967 at page 42.

CHAPTER V

CASE STUDIES

I have previously mentioned a number of elements as prerequisites in deciding upon and carrying through a merger. <u>To these, one must add a clear and honest evaluation of the status and conditions of one's own company, its financial strength as well as its limitations.</u>

The eventual formula for a merger or acquisition must start with a study of the other party's interest. Is there one controlling factor? What will be the public and shareholders' reactions? Is it going to be a tax-free merger or a taxable transaction? Should there be a voluntary tender or a stockholders' vote?

These questions must be answered first before any formula can be developed.

If it is to be a tax-free merger, then the issuance of common or preferred stock has to be used. If a taxable transaction is called for, then either cash or deferred payments or a combination of both might be called for. Further, will the vote be to merge, or will it be a vote to sell the assets with the sale to be followed by liquidation and distribution, or should there be creation of a holding company for the sellers? More often, in order to avoid annoying delays one might prefer giving stockholders a voluntary exchange offer or a voluntary tender for cash. As a rule, the latter will produce the same effect in the end, but it may take a little longer.

1. Rapid Electrotype's acquisition in September of 1955 may serve as an illustration of the above in several respects. Its purpose was to establish a base for future acquisitions and therefore the company had to possess the following elements:

a. Small enough capitalization so that it would not take too much money to buy control.

b. A profitable business and a steady earning capacity so that it might not disintegrate with a new controlling interest.

c. A good professional management to continue and a product line that was not dependent on one or two major customers.

d. No debt of any size and substantial excess cash so that it might lend itself to more borrowing to finance another acquisition.

e. Ability to buy control from insiders so that even if a premium should have to be paid, it would not arouse the enmity of the "powers" in control, leading to a prolonged fight, which might not always be successful and might ruin the company in the process.

Rapid Electrotype possessed the above elements. (See Table I, page 9.

1. It had 124,000 shares outstanding;

   Book Value $22 a share;

   Market Price $18 a share.

2. Its management was professional and diversified in five different cities. Except for the chairman of the board, the others did not own much of its equity.

   Its business was well distributed between hundreds of accounts in different parts of the country. It was a service business, and therefore, it had no inventory or large fixed assets.

   Its profits were quite steady and its five years' record was:

   1954 - $309,000   1953 - $377,000

   1952 - $240,000   1951 - $270,000   1950 - $415,000

3. No debt and a very substantial excess of cash was accumulated with no need for plant modernization and large expenditures on fixed investments.

4. Control rested in the hands of a seventy year-old man with no heirs. His natural desire would be to become more liquid. The other elements in

management could become allied with a group if they did not fear for their employment.

With the above analysis and my satisfaction as to the answer came the important question:

What should I offer to pay?

I recognized that not only would we have to pay cash, because this was the one thing that we had, but that we would have to pay a substantial premium and make the same offer to all shareholders. The reason for this was that I was an unknown entity in the financial field and the seller would not want to encounter any legal obstacles.

Every acquisition poses the difficult question of how much to pay and the answer is usually not very simple to reach. One does not want to pay too much for something that could be bought for less or offer less than what will buy it. One also faces the risk that if he offers less than what the seller wants, the offer may cause the seller to look elsewhere for a buyer or accept another offer; for he has now been aroused to the possibility of selling and will react quickly to a better offer.

It is for this reason that I usually like to find out first what will satisfy the seller and to know that for the moment I am the only one in the arena, while the seller hopes to get his price from me.

My analysis concerning the offering price for control of Rapid Electrotype ran somewhat like this:

I noted the excess cash per share which equalled almost the market price of $17. If I deducted this amount from the book value of the company, it would leave the business still capable of earning approximately $200,000 or more after taxes and therefore command an additional value of about $1,000,000 to $1,500,000, or an additional $11 to $16 per share. Knowing that not all the shares would be tendered, I reached the figure of $28 as an attractive price from my point of view and a figure probably acceptable to the seller.

The deal was finally concluded on the basis of $28 a share, which was the figure that was presented. A total of 40,000 shares were tendered and the price never went below the offering price. My guess was that it was because of the hopes that the other shareholders had of the potential growth of the company under its new leadership.

H. L. Green had purchased the control of United Stores in February 1959 for about $7 million in cash which was financed by short-term bank borrowings. By January 31, 1960 only $1 million had been repaid to the banks against its United Stores investment. It was clear from the outset that the price for the United Stores block would be $7 million as the directors of H.L. Green had to be made whole, or otherwise they would not vote the sale.

In review, we purchased for cash 363,000 shares of common stock of United Stores and 261,000 shares of $4.20 preferred stock. The allocation of cost is about $4,000,000 for the common and $3,000,000 for the preferred. The $4.20 preferred was non-cumulative with a liquidation value of $75 a share. It therefore had a book value of $85,000,000 but market value of the entire issue was about $12,000,000. Ahead of this preferred was the 6% preferred with a total market value of about $9,000,000. The market value of the McCrory McLellan stock and other assets was about $20,000,000.

Liabilities	6% pfd.	$ 9,000,000
	4.2% pfd.	12,000,000
	Total	$21,000,000
Assets		$20,000,000
Left for Common		($1,000,000)

How do you justify, then, paying $4,000,000 for the shares of common that represented only 70 percent of that issue, when the total issue was "under water"?

Without a recapitalization, United Common Stock clearly had no value, but I naturally looked beyond the holding company to its affiliate - McCrory McLellan - and to the merger that would eliminate this entire issue of 4.20 preferred. The balance sheet of McCrory McLellan was extremely strong. See Column 1 of Table VII, page 29. It had a total common equity of $56,000,000 and no debt. This was about $10,000,000 more than the market value that I assigned the proportionate shares owned by United Stores. When combined with BTL, we would make up the deficit paid for the common stock of United Stores and have a total equity of almost $100 million and virtually no debt. Such a merger would also fulfill BTL's objective of putting its funds to work in an operating company rather than maintaining BTL as as investment company.

    2. Oklahoma Tire and Supply Company offers an insight into the negotiations and successful conclusion of an acquisition of a privately owned company presenting the following characteristics:

        a. The asking price was quite high with very little possible variation.

b. The selling stockholders were mainly the management of the enterprise. Their good will, therefore, had to be preserved so as to cause little interruption and assure the pattern of normal growth.

c. Acquisition was important for McCrory since it was the only sizeable company left in its industry that had not already been acquired by a major concern.

Oklahoma Tire and Supply showed a very nice pattern of growth at the rate of about 10% increase in sales and earnings a year. Its management was considered to be the best in the industry. But despite earnings of about $1,900,000 after taxes, its book value was only about $14,000,000 and the asking price was $28,000,000. See Table XI, page 57.

There was no room for any creative construction of value for the sellers; they insisted on getting paid in money. Even the most optimistic multiple of their earnings could not justify the payment of their price; as a matter of fact, anything over $23 to 24 million would be overpricing it.

However, after a study of their blance sheet, I found that it was possible to generate $10,000,000

TABLE XI

OKLAHOMA TIRE AND SUPPLY COMPANY

BALANCE SHEET
AS OF 12/31/59
(in $ millions)

ASSETS

CURRENT ASSETS:

Cash	1.3
Accounts Receivable	9.4
Inventories	6.3
Prepaid Expenses	.1
Total Current Assets	17.0
Deferred Collections	.2
Net Plant	2.4
TOTAL	19.6

LIABILITIES

CURRENT LIABILITIES:

Long-Term Debt Due Within 1 Year	.1
Accounts Payable - Trade & Other	1.0
Accrued Liabilities	1.6
Total Current Liabilities	2.8
Long-Term Debt	.6
Deferred Federal Income Taxes	1.8
Common Stock & Surplus	14.4
TOTAL	19.6

from their assets by selling the accounts receivable that were created from their time sales and thus make the down payment from Oklahoma's own cash resources while paying the balance from their own profits. We incorporated a credit subsidiary and sold $8,000,000 of the receivables to this subsidiary; we also used $2,000,000 of their excess cash and were able to make a down payment of $10,000,000. The balance of $18,000,000 was contracted to be paid over a ten-year period.

The interest cost on sale of the receivables was to be borne by this division which also paid all interest charges for the use of any temporary loans to finance the inventory at its peak period. These additional charges amounted to about $650,000 before taxes. The interest cost to the parent company amounted to $950,000 for the first year and reduced $95,000 each year.

Based on the price of $28,000,000 and earnings of $2,200,000 before tax, it was simple arithmetic to see that the cost of interest would reduce earnings pre-tax to $1,600,000 or about $800,000 after tax. This might mean that McCrory would have to invest some additional money in payment of the debt, but over a period of years it would own Oklahoma Tire for nothing. Table XII shows what actually transpired in the following five years.

TABLE XII

RECONCILIATION OF McCRORY'S COST FOR OKLAHOMA TIRE & SUPPLY PLUS CASH FLOW DERIVED FROM OKLAHOMA: 1960 to 1965

(In $ Thousands)

Year	Pre-Tax Earnings	After-Tax Earnings	Excess Amortization	Total Cash Generated	McCrory's Net Interest Cost	McCrory's Payout	Total Expense	Net Annual Cash Generated	Net Cash Generated Cumulative
*1960	2,400	1,150	100	1,250	125	-	125	1,125	1,125
1961	3,100	1,510	400	1,900	500	1,800	2,300	(400)	725
1962	3,400	1,650	375	2,025	450	1,800	2,250	(225)	500
1963	3,800	1,900	350	2,250	400	1,800	2,200	50	550
1964	4,100	2,050	325	2,375	350	1,800	2,150	225	775
1965	4,450	2,250	300	2,550	300	1,800	2,100		1,225

NOTE: (*) Applies to October-December Only

We chose to write off some of the assets when we liquidated this subsidiary into the McCrory Corporation and depreciated them accordingly.

Thus, after five years, what looked like an exceedingly steep price showed the making of an excellent deal, with no investment of cash the company acquired was able to grow and pay out of its own earnings the cost of its acquisition, including interest and capital.

If all goes well, one may expect that in the next five years the company will generate some fifteen million dollars after taxes from earnings alone, while the capital payout and the interest after taxes will amount to about $10,000,000 for a net cash generation of $5,000,000.

3. <u>Lerner Stores</u> - The use of various techniques in making an acquisition is what, so to say, makes for "horse racing". As shown in the acquisition of Lerner Stores Corporation, the use of a "market" package, which included the creation of value for the seller well above its then market value, was the attraction to the management block of stock.

The stock of the company was selling on the New York Stock Exchange for about $23. There were 1,250,000 shares outstanding, of which the management controlled about 10%. There were two other blocks of stock of about 100,000 shares each; one was very friendly to the management while the other was the antithesis - though it never caused any problems.

I was very interested in this acquisition for the reasons that were previously mentioned, but I knew that only an attractive offer would move its management to take favorable action. They were very conscientious in their desire to give their shareholders the best possible deal and at the same time anxious to maintain the continuity of their management.

So it was up to me to come up with an offer that would provide the answers. Even though our company possessed the cash to make a good offer, I realized that a "good offer" might not be enough in this case. I also considered the future value of our cash in McCrory Corporation as too important to be dissipated and at the same time I considered our common or convertible preferred stock as too valuable to pay with at its then low market price. Short-term debt was also excluded from my considerations because we had just committed $18,000,000 worth of ten-year debt for the net acquisition cost of Oklahoma Tire and Supply.

The only way left was to pay with long-term debt which would call for small payouts for a number of years, increasing with time and ballooning at the end of fifteen years. It was obvious, however, that such a debenture would sell at a discount from its face value, and if I considered this discount of 10% or 15% in the price, the face value of the bond would be too high. This difference in relation to book value would be burdensome when the time came for our auditors to consider whether it should be amortized or preserved as a "good will" item on our balance sheet. Book value of Lerner's common stock at the time (1960) was about $28.

An additional sweetener was required here to balance the difference between the market value of the debenture and its face value, but it had to be created as a marketable commodity without penalizing the issuer. Warrants were utilized for this purpose.

Warrants, in essence, are a call on the common stock for a specified number of years and usually at a higher price than the stock is selling for. Their value is determined by considerations of the length of the call and the premium over selling price of the common stock. If the future looks bright for the company, they usually sell for a higher premium. Warrants are also very attractive from a trading point of view because they are less expensive to buy and are, therefore, much in demand by the speculators. The law of supply and demand helps their price quotation.

Warrants, however, tend sometimes to limit the demand for the common stock and therefore the price of the warrant too, because they offer another vehicle for participation in the future of the company; but at the time of their issue they do not dilute the earnings per share, and when they are exercised, they bring cash to the company's treasury.

Our stock was selling at the time at about $16 a share, and the warrants were to be exercised at $20 a share.

We offered the package of a $40 face value debenture with one warrant and a half to buy the stock at $20 for the same length as the debenture. Valuing the debenture at $34 (15% from face) and the warrant and a half at $9 to $10, the "package" worth came to over $40 a share.

With the announcement of this acquisition and the market of McCrory's common stock moving up, the warrant price moved even higher and the total package became more attractive so that the eventual tender to all shareholders brought in excess of 90% of the stock.

The total price paid in debentures was about $42,000,000, and about $3,500,000 in cash for one of the non-management blocks of stock plus a little over 1,500,000 warrants to buy McCrory shares at $20 a share for fifteen years.

Earnings of Lerner's, after taxes, were down slightly the year before, but recovered to around $3,400,000 in 1960. We paid, therefore, a price equal to thirteen times earnings.

Lerner continued to do well in the following five years and earnings topped $6,000,000 after taxes in 1965. Financially, Lerner Stores have accumulated in the five years earnings after taxes an amount of over $21,000,000. Because Lerner Stores always remained a subsidiary, its cash was transferred to the parent company through dividends that totalled about $26,000,000.

The cost of investment in cash was increased by about $8,000,000 through the acquisition of $9,000,000 worth of debentures (bought at about 10% discount) and interest costs in the past five years after taxes, were about $6,000,000 for a total cash cost of about $17,500,000.

In January 1966 we distributed about $8,500,000 worth of their stock and rights to our McCrory's stockholders and also sold 40% of the Lerner stock owned by McCrory for about $18,000,000.

Thus, on the balance sheet of McCrory Corporation - five years after it was first acquired, the cash results look somewhat like this:

<u>Expended</u>: $3,500,000 - Cash on purchase

                8,000,000 - Acquisition of debentures

                6,000,000 - Interest, after taxes (1961-1965)

             $17,500,000 - Total Cash Investment

<u>Received</u>: $26,000,000 - Dividends

                9,000,000 - Taxes refunded to parent company[1]

              18,000,000 - Sale of Lerner Stock

            $53,000,000 - Total Cash Generated

              8,500,000 - Distributed to the McCrory's shareholders

            $61,500,000 - Total cash generated and distributed

Remaining on our balance sheet as a liability were the $36,000,000 of debentures at face value. The market of Lerner's stock is about $20,000,000.[2] However, it must be noted that we have had a number of bids to sell this stock for over $30,000,000. Thus it can be said that our investment's true value is more or less equal to McCrory Corporation's carrying cost. In addition, an already realized profit, in cash, amounts to over

---

[1] Lerner continued to reserve for taxes on its own corporate books, but McCrory Corporation consolidated for tax purposes with all its subsidiaries and collected in cash the tax reserved by Lerner on its own books.

[2] The market value of the debentures is a little under $30,000,000

$35,000,000 exclusive of the distribution value, and $53,000,000 including this distribution.

From the standpoint of cash flow, the dividends being received from Lerners now almost equal, after taxes, the interest cost of the debentures still outstanding, while sinking fund requirements have been satisifed for at least three or four more years.

From the standpoint of earnings, based on present ownership of 50 percent of Lerner after interest reductions, Lerner contributes forty cents a share[3] to McCrory's earnings besides the value and income from the already realized cash of about $35,000,000.

I would consider this a most successful classic use of long-term debt and warrants in an acquisition of substantial size and stature, paying a very high price but benefiting accordingly.

---

[3] See Table XIII for calculations.

TABLE XIII

LERNER STORES CORPORATION

PROJECTED CONTRIBUTION TO McCRORY
Year Ending 1/31/67

Estimated Net Income	$7.0 Million
Less:	
Minority Interest	$3.5 Million
Debt Service	<u>1.0</u> Million
	$4.5 Million
Contribution To McCrory	<u>$3.5</u> Million
Contribution To McCrory Per Share	<u>$0.68</u>

Table XIV represents the structure of our interlocking corporate ownership.

The first circle - <u>Rapid American Corporation</u> - is the parent company. The one substantial business it owns in terms of size, is Joseph H. Cohen & Sons, Inc. The purpose of Rapid American is to assure the control and ownership of McCrory and to generate in the process the cash for the payments of its debt.

Because of a favorable tax treatment of dividends and because of the tax treatment of the interest, which is deductible, Rapid generates for tax purposes a loss against the operation of Joseph H. Cohen. This loss is in addition to losses accumulated in the same fashion in the past and also by the liquidation of the mail order and metal division in 1963.

In the event that Joseph H. Cohen should earn anywhere between $4,000,000 to $5,000,000 million a year, it would still require another acquisition with earnings of about $2,000,000 before taxes to fully utilize the tax loss.

Rapid American becomes most important in its ability to control such a vast company as McCrory and in turn the other companies that are a part of McCrory.

<u>McCrory Corporation,</u> the second circle, represents mainly a retail complex, with four different divisions in the retail field: variety stores (MMG), women's wear specialty stores

TABLE XIV

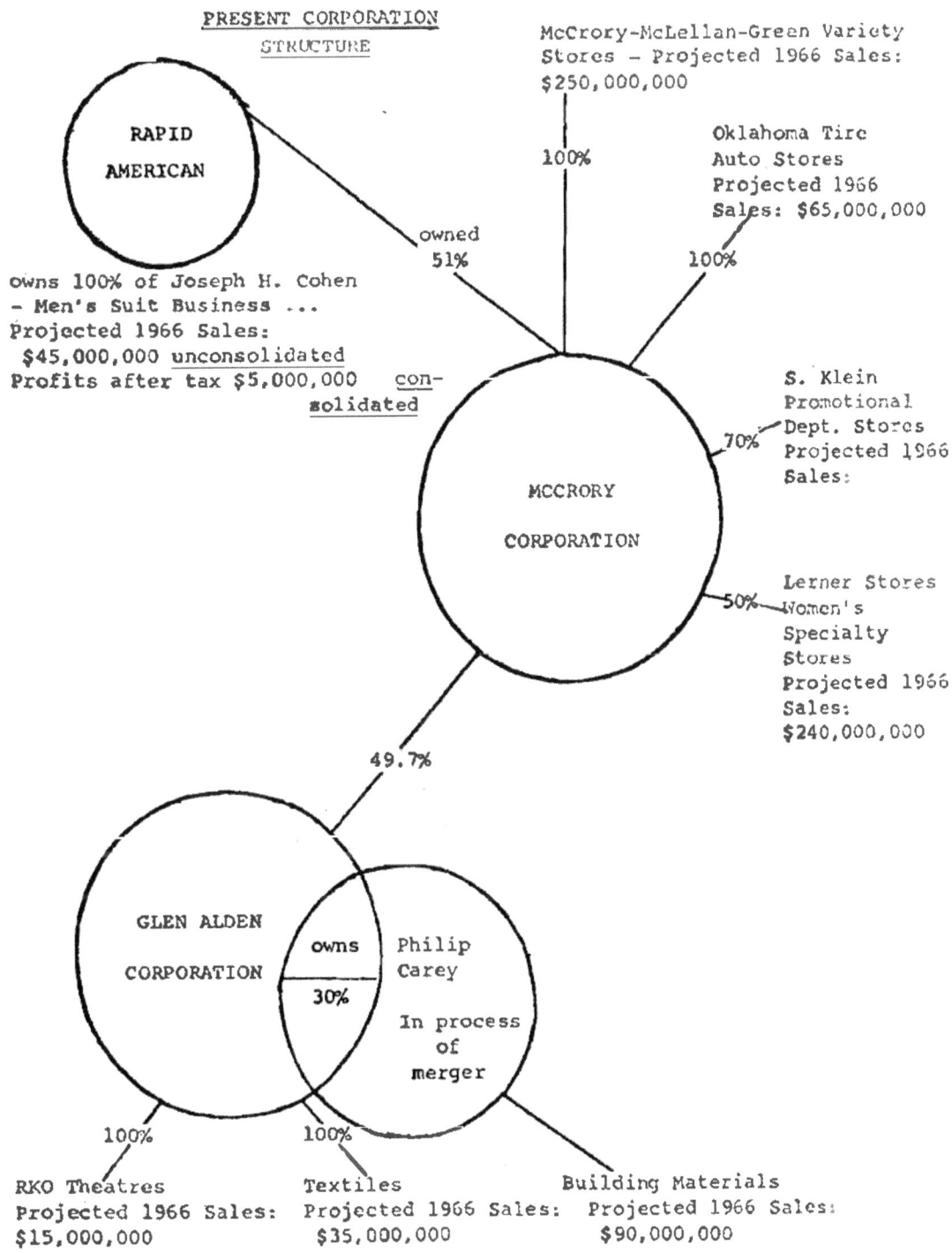

(Lerner), promotional department stores (S.Klein Department Stores, Inc.) and automotive stores (OTASCO).

This organization of a non-food retail complex is now completed and will concentrate its efforts on the improvement and expansion of both sales and profits. The greatest emphasis will be on S.Klein, where plans are now under developement for doubling the present number of stores and the total sales of the division. McCrory-McLellan-Green, too will be expanded at an accelerated tempo. Both Lerner and Otasco will continue their present satisfactory rate of expansion and growth.

Consolidated sales of this retail concern are now over $700,000,000 and will push in the next three to four years to reach $1,000,000,000. Its profits are aimed at a margin, after taxes, of 2% on sales.

Such a program will place McCrory among the top ten retailing (non-food) companies in the country behind Sears, Penny, Montgomery Ward, Woolworth and Federated, but alongside Allied, May, Kresge, Grant and Korvette.

McCrory's second function is to hold the reins of still another company that will concentrate on a diversification and investment policy. That company is Glen Alden Corporation.

Glen Alden Corporation - the third circle, is to become the arm of further diversification. Presently, Glen Alden operates two businesses: the RKO Theatres and a textile complex which manufactures grey cotton goods and denim. Both divisions are very profitable and further expansion of both promises to make them even more profitable.

Through the merger with Philip Carey, a very reputable building materials company, and through the possible acquisition of Briggs Manufacturing Company,[4] a prime maker of bathroom fixtures and water heating tanks, Glen Alden Corporation should also become a major factor in the home building industry.

After the merger, the combined earnings of the three major divisions may reasonably reach before taxes to about $13,000,000 to $15,000,000.

The earnings, the ability to increase its debt, and the still untapped cash resources of Glen Alden of about $40,000,000 make it possible to diversify further and expand so as to increase its earnings substantially.

Its expansion may be undertaken in one or two ways or by a combination of both: by completely merging with a company or by ownership of 51% of its equity, allowing this subsidiary to continue its own program under its own management, but benefiting from it by consolidating its pro rata share of the earnings.

---

[4] Glen Alden now has an option to acquire over 65% of the common stock of Briggs while it supplies management to this company.

In conclusion, I would point out that the construction of these interlocking companies provide for:

a. effective control of the whole concern;

b. successful buildup of a homogeneous large retailing complex; and

c. diversification and further activity through a controlled subsidiary, not affecting the larger complex.

CHAPTER VI

SUMMARY AND CONCLUSIONS

The effect of good operating management as a base for the success of an acquisition and expansion program has been repeatedly mentioned as part of the story. It will suffice, therefore, to say again that without good operating management the entire exercise in expansion would have been futile. The greatest effort and care is necessary, as shown by my personal experience, if continued growth is to be achieved.

However, in reviewing the foregoing chapters, one cannot escape reaching the conclusion that with all the variety in nature and scope of the companies involved in the acquisition and merger program described in this thesis, there is a general pattern of financial management which is responsible for the ultimate success of the effort

It may be advisable before concluding the paper to place special emphasis on a number of points deserving greater consideration but which have hitherto been dealt with in a more general way.

Prerequisites Probably the most difficult task is to face the challenges that are inherent in expansion and adquisition programs. Anyone who is intent on building and expand his business by way of mergers must have:

1. A crystal clear view of the aim one wishes to attain
2. Careful preparation of the steps leading up to the goal.
3. Psychological self-control.

Unless a person is entirely dedicated to one idea, he will only wander around and not look in the right direction. We all know the first Euclidean axiom of arithmetic that the shortest distance between two points is a straight line. It has two poles, one to start from and one to go to. For example, from the moment I first started in business I was aware of the aim I was heading for and predicted that our company would have $1,000,000,000 in sales ten years from the time of first achieving control.

The road to the goal is fraught with dangers and disappointments and one has to know that he is liable to encounter tough competition and that only those who are well prepared in every way may hope to succeed. He has to reckon with the daily struggle in his endeavor to overcome difficulties and remove obstacles, whether it be in explaining to his own colleagues the advantages of a contemplated deal or in convincing the bankers and financial institutions of the soundness of the project and its beneficial result to the corporation. All this requires meticulous planning, clear vision and complete mastery of the presentation.

One also has to study very thoroughly the motives and needs of the party he negotiates with, if he is to reach a satisfactory conclusion of the deal. Negotiations take place between human beings, each having his own problems and his own ways. No deal can be successfully consummated without adjusting the terms to fit the seller's needs and the answer to his specific problems, nor without taking into account the fact that he will habitually be surrounded by "experts" and "advisers" who must also be convinced of the seller's benefits from the transaction. A negotiator must be able to analyze objectively the terms from the standpoint of the opposing team and all through the negotiation act with complete self-control. He must never be jealous of any benefits gained by the seller nor begrudge him any concessions agreed upon if he is to achieve the outcome he has in Mind

<u>Purpose</u> Mergers may serve several purposes, but they usually have one single aim at the start. That aim is to create a better and more rounded operation that can lead to more profitable results.

As to purposes, I have seen and participated in mergers designed to bring about financial strength; undertaken in order to acquire a strong management team; seeking to provide capital for further growth; intended to create a market for a product or services rendered by the parent company; seeking to diversify the operations of the parent company; aspiring to provide for a greater buying power in some area; endeavoring to utilize tax losses of the parent company; and sometimes endeavoring even to satisfy the fancies of the management and directors.

The profit motivation should of course be the main consideration. Without this, I would question the wisdom of the whole transaction.

Cash   As will be seen from reading the previous chapters, after the first acquisition of Rapid Electrotype, the determining factor in the success of all subsequent deals, has been effective use, or rather non-use, of cash.

The point of cash can best be illustrated by asking the question: "If you knew that I was in a position to pay for the article I wished to buy, would you give me credit? (The word "credit" here and throughout this thesis is to be understood as buying without paying, i. e., receiving loans and paying later.) Of course the answer is bound to be "**yes**", and vice-versa, if one did not have the cash to pay for the merchandise he wished to buy, he would certainly be required to pay cash.

This thought remained in my mind throughout the whole time and this was the underlying reason for my actions in the various acquisitions I made. Whenever possible, I called for an acquisition to be made without cash. If I had to pay cash, I projected the immediate generation of equivalent cash from the acquired company.

Unless the above was possible, I preferred not to go ahead with the deal. Time and again our group of companies stayed out of trouble by having one or another as a large holder of cash, commanding the respect and confidence of financial institutions.

In our negotiation for acquisition, we as a rule adjusted the terms to our corporate structure by having the seller know that we had the cash to pay. We did not have to resort to long term borrowings from insurance companies with their very strict rules. Instead we were able to issue our own long term debt or equity securities. In the cases of Oklahoma Tire and of Lerners Stores together, we issued $63,000,000 of long term debt.

When the full acquisition of H.L. Green was projected by McCrory Corporation, it was based in part on the consummated sale by H.L. Green of the Canadian division for cash and the re-generation of this cash into McCrory for the cash used in the tender for H.L. Green stock.

When McCrory's diversification program was to be initiated through Glen Alden, it took into account the fact that the $25,000,000 take-out initially required for Glen Alden commanded the use of at least that amount of cash in Glen Alden and twice that amount after further liquidation and cash generation.

Two other aspects are worth mentioning:

First - the reliance from time to time on raising cash via offers of debentures to our own shareholders or by offering to purchase a participation in a subsidiary company. The margin requirements or rights offerings are very favorable to those shareholders who exercise them. There is only a 25% margin required. Since our shareholders have benefited most of the time from the growth of the company, they have actively exercised these offerings. Using a method by which they were allowed to oversubscribe we never had to resort to investment bankers for the sale of our debt and so raised cash without the cost of underwriting.

Second - the elaborate system of financial controls that we prescribed for all our companies. We could tell at a glance how our divisions were doing by noting their cash flow. Even today reports of the actual cash and bank balances flow through our home office so that we can make effective use of cash or check actual receipts against projected cash flows.

In short, holding of cash gives rise to two advantages:

1. The confidence, respect and good relations with financial institutions, without whose support no management can operate effectively; and

2. The ability to expand and acquire without the use of cash.

In summary, capabilities in two arenas have played a predominant role in achieving the success as outlined herein: The ability to read the needs of the other party to the negotiations and know what will satisfy these needs and the constant effort to conclude the transactions without depletion of cash in the process.

BIBLIOGRAPHY

Donaldson, Gordon. *Corporate Debt Capacity*
    Boston: Harvard University Press, 1961

Drucher, Peter F. *The Practice of Management*
    New York: Harper & Brothers Publishers, 1954

Foulke, Roy A. *Practical Financial Statement Analysis*
    New York: McGraw-Hill Book Co., Inc., 1957

Graham, Benjamin
& Dodd, David T. *Security Analysis*
    New York: McGraw-Hill Book Co., Inc., 1951

Greenewalt, Crawford H. *The Uncommon Man*
    New York: McGraw-Hill Book Co., Inc., 1959

Hall, Stewart H. *Age of the Moguls*
    New York: Doubleday & Co., Inc., 1953

Morton, Frederich. *The Rothschilds*
    New York: Atheneum Publishers, 1962

Nevins, Allan &
Hill, Ernest. *FORD Expansion & Challenge 1915-1932*
    New York: Charles Scribner's Sons, 1957

Smith, Richard Austin. *Corporations in Crisis*
    New York: Doubleday & Co., Inc., 1963

Trescott, Paul B. *Financing American Enterprise*
    New York: Harper & Row, 1963

Weiss, E.G. *Merchandising for Tomorrow*
    New York: McGraw-Hill Book Co., Inc., 1961